THE

FUGITIVE SLAVE BILL;

OR,

GOD'S LAWS PARAMOUNT TO THE LAWS OF MEN.

A

SERMON,

Preached on Sunday, October 20, 1850,

BY REV. NATHANIEL COLVER,

Pastor of the Tremont St. Church.

PUBLISHED BY REQUEST OF THE CHURCH.

BOSTON:
J. M. HEWES & CO., 81 CORNHILL.
(Successors to John Putnam.)
1850.

RESOLUTIONS,

PASSED BY THE TREMONT STREET BAPTIST CHURCH, BOSTON, OCT. 11, 1850.

Whereas, God is supreme in legislation, and his laws imperative and binding upon all the subjects of his moral government; and

Whereas, No corporate body or earthly government, can by counter legislation, release him from, or justify him in disobeying the laws of God; and

Whereas, The entire system of American slave law, by which the slaves are reduced from men to chattels, and deprived of their liberty, is a flagrant and unmistakeable outrage upon the laws of God and upon the heaven bestowed rights of our common nature in the persons of the slaves; and

Whereas, The recently passed "Fugitive Slave Bill," is a part and parcel of the same atheistical code, and in direct and manifest opposition to the revealed will and law of God, who requires of us "To deliver him that is spoiled, out of the hand of the oppressor," "To hide the outcasts, and to bewray not him that wandereth," "To let his outcasts dwell with us," &c. And who also expressly forbids a compliance with this law, saying, "Thou shalt not deliver unto his master, the servant which is escaped from his master unto thee, he shall dwell with thee even among you, in that place which he shall choose, in one of thy gates where it liketh him best; thou shalt not oppress him." Therefore,

Resolved, That as disciples of Christ and members of his church, we ought not, we cannot, and as we fear God, we will not render obedience to the said law. We should regard it as practical atheism, for a moment to give it the supremacy over the law of God, with which it is at direct and manifest war.

We do indeed, recognize our duty with all meekness, to abide whatever penalties a wicked and oppressive government may see fit to inflict upon us for our fidelity to the laws of God. But be the consequences what they may, we feel solemnly bound by every means in our power, to feed, comfort, shelter and aid the fugitive from southern bondage, the same as if no such law existed, and the same as if they were our own children, fleeing from the savages of the wilderness, or from any enemy who was seeking feloniously to deprive them of their liberties or lives.

Resolved, That the alarm, consternation and distress, into which numerous families of our fellow citizens have been thrown by the aforesaid law, suspending as it does, "the writ," and "trial by jury," and thereby exposing even those who were never in bondage, to the perpetual doom of slavery, and connected as they are by ties of consanguinity with those who have escaped from slavery, or in part, or in whole, composed of such persons, demand the entire sympathy of all who fear God and love their fellow men.

Resolved, That we deeply deplore the recklessness of those legislators, who, by the passing of the aforementioned Bill, have precipitated this terrible crisis. They have placed the citizens in a position where they are compelled to defile their consciences, do violence to every humane and generous feeling of their hearts, and to knowingly sin against God, or refuse obedience to this law. They have done a fearful work; deeply do we deplore it, and earnestly will we pray God to save the country from the fearful results with which it is now threatened.

Resolved, After careful and prayerful deliberation, that the above preamble and resolutions be signed by the pastor and clerk, and published as the solemn convictions and purposes of this church.

NATHANIEL COLVER, *Pastor*.
JOSEPH J. HOWE, *Clerk*.

SERMON.

Acts 5 : 29.

THEN PETER AND THE OTHER APOSTLES ANSWERED AND SAID, WE OUGHT TO OBEY GOD RATHER THAN MEN.

SUBJECTION to the civil magistrate is a scriptural doctrine. "The powers that be, are ordained of God. Render unto Cæsar the things that are Cæsar's." Cæsar has his rights, and those rights God commands us to respect. His powers are given to him of God, and sanctioned of God. But the prerogatives of civil government are given for a certain end, and have their limitation. If its delegated powers be perverted to another end, or if it transcend its limits, its claims to respect cease to be sanctioned of God. If civil government in any form, forget the limitation of its prerogatives, and invade the prerogatives of God, it is at its peril. God is supreme in his legislation, and he whose mandate secures the rights of Cæsar, has also said, "and to God the things that are God's." God will claim his own, and no civil government can release its subjects from rendering unto God the things that are his. Our allegiance to civil government must be subordinate to our allegiance to the higher government of God, and hence, if at any time the claims of the one conflict with those of the other, the weaker must give place to the stronger, and the civil must yield to the divine.

God required the apostles to preach the gospel, saying, "Go, stand in the temple, and preach all the words of this life." The civil authorities forbade them,—commanding them to speak no more in that name. "Then Peter and the other apostles answered and said, we ought to obey God rather than men." The civil government had transcended the limits of its powers—nay, it arrayed its powers against the higher government from which it derived all its authority. Of course, in such a work, it could not continue to claim the sanction and support of that government while it was seeking its overthrow, nor could it be obeyed in such a work without offence to God. If any human government will venture upon so fearful an experiment, it must take the consequences. Under such circumstances, the duty of the subject cannot be doubtful. If he take counsel of his fears, he may hesitate; but if he take counsel of his duty, he will prefer the authority of God to the authority of men. Such a decision may be costly, but it will be just, and safe in the end.

The recent legislation of the Congress of the United States, in the enactment of the Fugitive Slave Bill, providing for the recapture of fugitives from Southern bondage, has placed the citizens of the free States in such a position. They are commanded to assist in its execution. With its strange and iniquitous provisions, humanity has been shocked. The feeling is almost universal, that its execution would be the commission of a monstrous crime. It has carried consternation and anguish into thousands of families in our midst, and its execution would doom thousands who are guilty of no crime, many of whom are the disciples of Christ, to a fate between which and death there would be but little if any choice. Under such circumstances, the inquiry has been bitter and earnest, what shall be done? what is our duty? To no class in community does this inquiry more appropriately appeal, than to the spiritual advisers in the church of God. With that appeal, as an ambassador of Christ, I dare not trifle. With a painful and trembling reluctance, I yield. I shrink with indescribable distress from the thought of seeming, for a moment, to counsel disobedience to the laws of the land. But when, on the other hand, it is obvious that a crime of appalling magnitude is about to be committed in the name of law—a crime involving the hopeless ruin of thousands—the conscience of the nation defiled and humanity outraged—I dare not be silent. In such a crisis, the witnesses of God are not at liberty to be silent. "If these should hold their peace, the stones would immediately cry out."

Brethren, pray for me, that I may be enabled to investigate the subject to which our attention is thus imperatively drawn, in such a manner as to subserve the best interests of truth, and to please the great Head of the church.

From the text I have selected, two propositions will be submitted for your consideration.

1st. *Whenever the law of any civil government demands of its subjects either active or passive disobedience to the known will, or law of God, disobedience to the former, in favor of the latter, becomes an imperative duty.*

Let the proposition be distinctly understood. I do not say that resistance to every unrighteous law is a duty. Laws may make very unrighteous and oppressive exactions upon us, and it may be our duty to submit. "If he sue thee at the law and take away thy coat, let him have thy cloak also." The exaction may be unjust and cruel, but it is to be borne. It is only when the law commands the subject to do that which the law of God forbids, or to fail to do that which the law of God commands, that he is bound to resist it. We shall greatly err if we do not keep this distinction constantly in view. This proposition, thus carefully defined, is sustained, I remark, in the first place, by men acting under the inspiration and approbation of God. The three worthies, mentioned in the third chapter of Daniel, afford a case in point. The law of God forbade idolatry; but idolatry had identified itself with the political affairs of Babylon. Nebuchadnezzar, the king, had constructed an image of great dimensions, cost and beauty. He had, by solemn edict, commanded the subjects of his empire to worship his idol. At that command, and with unsurpassed enthusiasm, his subordinates in office had rushed from the numerous provinces of his empire to testify their loyalty to their monarch, by doing homage to his god. How grateful to the pride of his heart must have been this profound submission to his will, this zealous obedience to his authority? On the other hand, how astonished and offended, to learn that that obedience was not universal. It was told him that three individuals of the captives of Judah had disregarded his authority. Men, too, who were the recipients of his imperial favor, and bound by the pledge of office, received from his hand, to sustain his government. That these men, in opposition to the congregated wisdom and virtue of the nation, had disregarded their own official obligations by setting at naught the solemn mandate of the king, and refusing to bow down and worship his god. As a godless politician, what could he see in all this but dangerous fanaticism, or stubbornness and revolt? It was quite natural, with the views which he entertained of the nature and extent of his own authority, that he should feel and act as he did. In his "rage" and his "fury," he commanded them to be brought before him. He charged them with their disloyalty, and warned them of the fatal results of their fanaticism. But he would not be unreasonable, he would even condescend that they should have an opportunity to redeem their reputation and save their lives. If at the second musical indication of his will, they would fall down and worship the image which he had set up, well,—the past should be forgiven and they should live; but if not, in that same hour they should be cast into the burning fiery furnace, which, in his wrath, he would cause to be seven times heated; and "who," he impiously added, "who is that God that shall deliver you out of my hand?" But there stood those three men, unmoved as the hills planted by the hand of Jehovah. They heard the threat, they saw the dangers with which they were surrounded. But moral courage dares to be afraid. They feared God and were unmoved. They heard the power of their God challenged, and they would not fail, through cowardice or treachery, to honor it with their confidence,—the observed of heaven, and a worthy spectacle to be looked back upon by all coming generations. There they stood, a noble specimen of manhood,—of manhood unsuborned from its high allegiance to its God, and unbowed by the glittering seductions of earth from its proper dignity. How amazing and how inspiring the contrast between them and the multitude of cringing sycophants with whom they were surrounded! Memorable indeed is the answer which they returned to this imperial encroachment upon their rights and duties as men. It is an answer worthy to be engraved upon the memory of the race, and to be had in readiness for every tyrant who should thus forget the limits of his authority, and thrust himself between men and their God. "Shadrach, Meshach and Abednego, answered and said to the king, O Nebuchadnezzar, we are not careful to answer thee in this matter. If it be so, our God, whom we serve, is able to deliver us from the burning fiery furnace. But, if not, be it known unto thee, O king, that we will not serve thy gods, nor worship the golden image which thou hast set up." What commendable fidelity to righteousness is here displayed! What moral dignity! What sublime faith in God! But to all this, this self-deified politician is blind. Their unseduced and unawed virtue serve only to augment his wrath.

"Then was the king full of fury, and the form of his visage was changed." The furnace was heated till it burned with seven fold fury! They were cast in. Pressed by the vehemence of his command, the executioners of his will were smitten down by the gushing flames from that overheated engine of his rage. Those feeble victims have been made to drink the full cup of his vengeance. His eye follows them that he may feast upon the dying agonies of their crisping bodies, as they should yield to the devouring element! But mark that king! Another change has come over his visage. Wonder, amazement and fear sit enthroned upon his pallid brow! What sight appals him? Those devouring flames have given them a kindly reception. That fiery furnace is changed into the audience chamber of the Great King, whose authority he has despised and whose power he has challenged. "The form of the fourth" is with them; he sees him as "the Son of God." Virtue has triumphed. Fidelity to God is vindicated. The Son of God himself has come down to honor those men who have dared to disobey the law of the king in favor of the higher law of their God. For once that proud monarch is humbled, and made to cast his crown at the feet of the sovereign God. The supremacy of divine legislation is established, and a confession of it is wrung from the lips of a tyrant. A confession which proclaims at once the guilt of his own usurpation, the vileness of his obsequious parasites, and the righteousness of those humble but faithful witnesses for God. In all this, the truth of our proposition is taught us, so clearly taught us as not to be mistaken. So authenticated by the divine interposition and so confirmed by this confession of the civil government, as to leave no room to doubt nor safety in hesitation.

There is a like confirmation of our proposition in the conduct of Daniel under the iniquitous law of Darius, with this difference. The law of Nebuchadnezzar required active, that of Darius passive disobedience to the law of God. The case is so much in point as to demand our careful attention, as it shows conclusively, that the man who truly fears God will not and cannot yield to the interposition of the civil law, between him and his God in the least particular, be the consequences what they may.

The law of Darius wanted nothing in form or sanction. The signature of the king was affixed to the decree. It was after the law of the Medes and Persians. It could neither be changed nor repealed. It required the commission of no crime against his fellow-men on the part of Daniel. It simply forbade his calling upon the name of his God. Daniel would neither obey, nor *seem* to obey it. He might have continued to call upon his God, and thus have foiled his enemies and avoided any liability to the terrible penalty of the law, by praying in secret. But in so doing he would seem either to yield to the right of the king to interfere between him and his God, or to distrust that God, whose servant he professed to be. He would do neither the one nor the other; but "When he knew that the writing was signed, he went into his house, and his windows being open in his chamber toward Jerusalem, he kneeled upon his knees three times a day, and prayed and gave thanks before his God, as he did aforetime." He was willing they should know that he disobeyed the mandate of the king. By the steady, unaltered manner in which he did it, he wished his enemies to know that he acted from no motive of resentment, but from his unshaken fidelity to his God and, his willingness to suffer for him if need be. For this disobedience to civil law in favor of the divine, God abundantly honored him. The angels of heaven were observant of the singular trial to which that servant of God was subjected. His entrance to that terrible receptacle of death was preceded by one, sent from the celestial world, to render it a place of safety and repose to the man "greatly beloved!" The piety of Daniel in this matter has deeply impressed the king. The very God of Daniel was apparent in his piety. The impressions of this heathen monarch were undoubtedly vague; but somehow he felt that Daniel's God was not a fiction, nor unmindful of his servant. Of this his night of fasting and his early visit to the den were indicative. "And when he came to the den, he cried with a lamentable voice unto Daniel: O Daniel, servant of the living God, is thy God whom thou servest continually, able to deliver thee from the lions?" Would he have cried thus had no confidence in Daniel's God impressed his mind? "Then said Daniel unto the king, O king, live forever. My God hath sent his angel, and hath shut the lions' mouths, that they have not hurt me; forasmuch as before him innocency was found in me; and also before thee, O king, have I done no hurt." He had studiously disobeyed the law, but he had done no hurt. His own conscience approved; God, by miracle, had approved. The king feels it, and adds his own testimony. His confession on that memorable occasion of the supremacy of the kingdom of God, is an everlasting commendation of the truth of our proposition.

In disobeying the law of the king in favor of the will of God, Daniel is fully sustained. On the truth of our proposition, patriarchs, prophets and apostles, have all acted. To deny it, is to stamp all the holy martyrs of every age with suicidal folly. All of them have died for disobedience to some civil law—to some law which required them actively or passively to disobey the will of God. If our proposition be untrue, they have died as the fool dieth. We ought to obey God, rather than men, has been their dying apology.

But again, the very existence of God, pledges the truth of our proposition. The "I AM" of the Bible claims to be "God above all gods." He claims to be "King (not among, but) *above* all gods." "His kingdom ruleth *over* all." He claims no equality of being or of rule. Supremacy of authority is essential to his existence as God. To deny the supremacy of his laws, is to deny his existence as God. The recent contemners of the higher law, whether in the Congress of the United States or among the apologists and advocates of this Bill, are practical atheists. I mean those who admit the injustice of its provisions, and yet say it should be obeyed because it is the law of the land. If the subjects of the moral government of God can be released from their obligation to obey the law, or known will of God in one case by the authority of civil law, then they can be released in another, and in all cases, and the government of God is at an end. To perpetuate crimes of any enormity with impunity, yea, with justice, you have only to find some human government vile enough to command the commission of such crimes, and they are changed at once into virtues. And yet, from this monstrous conclusion there is no escape but in the truth of the proposition we have been laboring to establish, and which, it seems to me, we have succeeded in establishing beyond the possibility of a doubt. The man that truly fears God, will hold his will, his law supreme, and his obligations to regard it as sacred and inviolable. As these obligations are personal, and as no being in the universe can step between him and his God, or bear his responsibilities for him, he will examine every law of men which lays claim to his regard, and if it demand active or passive disobedience to the will or law of his God, he ought to disobey it, and he will disobey it.

We proceed to submit the second proposition for your consideration, viz:—*Such is the inherent and manifest iniquity of this Bill, such its hostility to the law of God, as to render disobedience to its demands a solemn duty.*

Of course we shall attempt no minute or detailed examination of this strange and afflictive Bill. We can only notice some of its more prominent features, by which it is entitled to be disobeyed and repudiated by every freeman in the land.

And first—Obedience to this Bill will render us the efficient and direct responsible supporters of slavery itself.

I need not, I am quite sure, in this assembly stop to prove the inherent vileness of slave law, based as the entire code is, upon an atheistical invasion of the divine prerogatives. "Slaves shall be deemed, held, taken and reputed to be goods and chattels personal, in the hands of an owner, to all intents, purposes and constructions whatsoever. Slaves shall not be reckoned among sentient beings, but among things. A slave can neither plead nor be pleaded for; he cannot be known in law, save in the person of his master or owner."—(South Carolina Slave Law). "And this," says Judge Stroud, "is the basis of all slave law, wherever slavery exists in this country." By these quotations any one can perceive that slavery begins its cruel work upon its victim by legally nullifying his manhood, with all its *peculiar* rights and prerogatives; by metamorphosing the man into a mere animal, "a thing." Well might Wesley denominate such a system "the sum of all villany." He who denies its vileness, perpetrates a libel upon his own powers of perception. Let the attempt be made to apply it to himself, or to his own children, and will he longer profess his blindness to its appalling enormity? If there be any sin of surpassing offensiveness to a holy God, it is the shameless attempt to prostitute his precious word to its defence. Now, terrible as is the iniquity of this system in all its practical cruelties and legitimate results, obedience to this Bill will make us the direct and efficient supporters of it. You cannot separate the slave catcher from the slave holder. The commencement and continuance of the outrage upon the victim, results from the conspiracy between the two; so that, both the catcher and the holder, are alike involved in the guilt. Fully to perceive this, you have only to suppose your own child the victim.

Some person at the South has possession of your child, and subjects him to the degradations and cruelties of slavery.

Panting for liberty, your child succeeds in making his escape. Just as he reaches your dwelling, and while yet clasped in your affectionate embrace, (under the provisions of this Bill, and in obedience to its mandate,) your neighbor, with the eager stealthiness of the tiger, seizes upon your child, and bears him back to his Southern oppressor, to toil, suffer and groan, till death comes to his release. How would you regard that neighbor? Would you not regard him as equally cruel to your child, as equally involved in the guilt of his enslavement, as equally responsible in the sight of God for his condition and suffering? The authors of this Bill have sought to make the free citizens of the North the guilty participants in the sin of slavery; the efficient abettors and supporters of that system of unsurpassed iniquity—of that quintessence of all cruelties—that "sum of all villanies!" And there is no way for us to avoid it, but by disobedience to the Bill. If we would be clear, we must repudiate it, as "part and parcel" of the God-defying code of American slavery.

But again. This Bill demands a palpable and flagrant violation of that universal and indispensable law of life, pressed upon us by the express command of our Lord; "Therefore, all things whatsoever ye would that men should do to you, do ye even so to them; for this is the law and the prophets."

The trembling fugitive in this city, whose head this terrible Bill has uncovered, and to whom it points as its victim, is your neighbor. He has escaped from the dark prison-house of slavery, where he was held against all right, all justice. For a time, he has breathed the free air of New England, and shared its civil, its domestic and its religious privileges. Beyond the reach of the spoiler, whose avarice sucked up the marrow of his youth, he has felt himself secure until this Bill commanded his neighbors to seize him, and take him back to the horrors from which he had escaped. Will you be the one to do it, or assist in doing it? Put yourself in his place, and would you wish him to do it to you? In deference to any principle of justice, ought you to wish him to do it? In the most *self-sacrificing* exercise of Christian love, *could you* desire him to do it to you?

If you would, if you ought, if you could, then obey this Bill. Set about it in earnest. Heed not the tears, the anguish, the shrieks, the despair of bruised and crushed humanity. Let not the sundered ties, the grief-tossed limbs, the breaking hearts which will strew your way, deter you; press on, and do your duty! But if not, then with that firmness which becomes the upright and God-fearing, say to the authors of this Bill, we will not obey it. In honor of our Saviour, and of that beautiful law of universal application which dropped from his lips, we will not obey this unrighteous decree. Despite the enormous penalties of this Bill, we will obey our Saviour. Our brother shall dwell quietly by our side, and we will do him good.

But again. Obedience to this Bill, involves an outrage upon every law of hospitality to the stranger, and of charity to the needy, which the gospel enjoins; as well as upon every generous, manly, or religious prompting of the heart.

The fugitive comes to us, not in the exuberances of wealth, wherewith to bless and protect himself. He comes from the hand of the spoiler. Espionage upon his soul has enfeebled his mind. The keen discipline of the lash has scarified his flesh. His solitary griefs have wounded his spirit. Unceasing toil has bowed his frame, and "his feet they hurt in fetters." The earnings of his hands have been taken to increase the wealth of his oppressors, while he has been left in his poverty. He comes, not to bless, but to be blest; but he comes as the representative of Jesus Christ. These marks of his woe are his legible credentials. Sealed with the King's signet, he comes to us a clearly written draft upon the charity of our hearts, and the benevolence of our hands. We cannot dishonor this draft without grieving our Lord. He will feel it as if done to himself. *Their* necessities are *his* claims, appealing to the tenderest and holiest sensibilities of our natures. But what does this Bill? Like a polar frost, it nips the first buddings of humanity. In the icy fingers of its grasp, it locks all our energies. It lays its injunction upon all the moral wealth of the soul. It counsels treason to all the tender commands—to all the earnest injunctions of the Son of God.

Not having the fear of this law before their eyes, humanity and charity have begun, at least, to do their work. Many of these fugitive remnants of humanity, wrecked upon the dark and rock-bound coast of slavery, have been allowed to find a home among us. Under the genial sky of freedom, the cramped energies of their souls have begun to expand. Their drooping hearts have sent out their tendrils, and taken hold of the props of social life. The weary anguish of their spirits has found rest in the humble but sacred retreats of domestic affection, and a chosen home. But what says this Bill? Why, this is all a mistake. This work must be undone. These new-born ties that bind them to life must all be sundered. These expanding energies must again be crushed. These homes must be desolated, and this newly risen sun of their hopes must be made to set forever in the mornless night of renewed slavery! Surely, this is not a work for men, but demons! And yet, this is the very work which this monster, begotten upon ambition, by the warring winds of political strife, prescribes for the free citizens of the North—for the freemen of Massachusetts!

But further. Obedience to this Bill involves a direct violation of many, very many of the moral precepts of the Bible. God says, "Hide the outcasts." This Bill says, hide them at your peril. God says, "Betray not him that wandereth;" but this Bill commands you to betray him into the hands of his worst enemy. God says, "Suffer mine outcasts to dwell with you;" this Bill says, enter their humble dwellings, seize them, call out the *posse comitatus*, carry them out of the State, and deliver them to the scourge, to the shambles or to death, as the unbridled caprice of their oppressors shall determine.

God says:—"Thou shalt not deliver to his master the servant which is escaped from his master unto thee; he shall dwell with thee, even among you in that place which he shall choose, in one of thy gates where it liketh him best; thou shalt not oppress him." This Bill takes direct issue with

God and says, YOU SHALL DELIVER HIM TO HIS MASTER!

It commands every citizen of the North to disregard the expressed will of his God. This alternative has been thrust upon us with a recklessness that is amazing. The authors of this Bill have taken issue with God. To yield obedience to the claims of both is impossible. Neutrality is impossible. There remains therefore to the upright but one decision, and that is the decision of the apostle in our text,—"*We ought to obey God rather than men.*"

As we would avoid doing violence to all the generous promptings of humanity, or of Christianity, in our hearts we must disobey and repudiate this Bill. As we would avoid doing violence to all the moral precepts of the Bible, we must disobey and repudiate this Bill. In short, as we would avoid renouncing the moral government of God or incurring the wrath of heaven, we must disobey and repudiate this Bill.

But again:—This Bill should be abhorred and trampled under foot by every man, because it enjoins the commission of one of the blackest crimes specified in the divine catalogue. A crime which is thus classified by an inspired apostle,—"Murderers of fathers, murderers of mothers, MAN-STEALERS." "He that stealeth a man and selleth him, or if he be found in his hand, he shall surely be put to death." But let us examine somewhat carefully, and see if this terrible crime is involved in obedience to this Bill.

What, then, constitutes the crime of man-stealing? Is it to take one man from another who claims to be his owner? By no means. To take him from such a claimant is but to release him from a felonious seizure. How came that professed *owner* by that immortal being, who bears the image of his Maker, to whom he is bound by ties as indissoluble as his nature,—ties based upon the right of his Maker to his unfettered service? Before that professed owner can vindicate himself from a felony upon the rights and possession of God, he must show his bill of sale or his title deed from his owner, and his owner is God. To deliver or to release every slave in all the South from the felonious ownership of their oppressors, would no more be man-stealing than when Abraham delivered Lot and his fellow-captives out of the hands of the five kings who claimed them as the spoil taken in war. To give freedom to all the slaves of the South would be no more man-stealing, than for the noble Decatur to give liberty to American captives who had been taken by the Algerine powers and reduced to slavery. Upon those who could effect such a deliverance, Melchizedek would pronounce the blessing of the most high God. Whatever else may be man-stealing, to release the slaves of the South is not man-stealing. Even the slaveholder himself is barred by slave law against such a complaint. The very basis of all slave laws declares that he (the slave) is not to be regarded as a man; "He shall not be reckoned among sentient beings, but among things." He does not profess to own him as a man but as a thing. The rights of the slave, as a man, would perpetually war upon every prerogative of ownership in his master. It surely is not for him who has annihilated his manhood, that he may *own* him, to revive that manhood as a plea against him who has released his spoiled victim and restored him to his manhood again. Such a release is no man-stealing; it is an act of mercy, in obedience to God, who says, "Thou shalt deliver him that is spoiled out of the hand of the oppressor."

The question returns, what is it to steal a man? We answer, in order to steal property, it must be taken from a rightful owner. So in order to steal a man, he must be feloniously taken away from his rightful owner; or, in either case, it will be the same thing, if the article or the man be taken from the official agent, in whom the owner had vested the right of control. Now we have no fear of contradiction when we affirm that God is the rightful owner of man, and that he has constituted every man his agent, vested with the exclusive power over all his own faculties and responsible to God for their use. So sacred is this agency of the Divine owner, that no man can relinquish it or cast from him its obligations. He received it at his birth, and he can only relinquish it with his being. His responsibilities to his God constitute the inalienable character of his rights. It was the sacredness of this trust that led the apostles to say, "We ought to obey God rather than men." It has been the sacredness of this trust which has led every martyr to die rather than relinquish it. Now he who takes a man out of this moral relationship to his God, and reduces him to the relations of a mere chattel and steps between God and him and claims to be his owner, he it is that steals a man. There can be no more truthful definition of the crime of man-stealing than the reducing of a *man* to the legally defined condition of a slave.

To seize a man in the jungles of Africa, and bind him as your slave, is man-stealing. It is to reduce a man to a chattel which constitutes the crime; and when the Virginia or South Carolina planter buys that stolen man, he buys a felonious title, and while he holds him or owns him, he does it under a felonious title and in violation of the rights of God and the slave, and thus he perpetuates the crime of man-stealing. In the case of the descendants of the slave, who are by him held in slavery, he does but multiply and perpetuate the crime of man-stealing. The title of man-stealer is written by the finger of Almighty God upon the brow of every man who claims to be the OWNER of a MAN, or who subjects him to his uses as a mere chattel.

Well, from the felonious grasp of a human owner the fugitive among us has escaped. He has come to breathe the free air of New England, where, unfettered by the oppressive ownership of another, he can yield obedience to his rightful proprietor, the blessed God. He has come where he can "Honor his father and his mother;" where he can cherish and protect the wife of his bosom; where he can train up his "Children in the nurture and admonition of the Lord." He has come where he can give himself to "Search the Scriptures," and to "feed on the bread of life," or to the service of God, as duty may demand. He has come where, in short, under the genial influence of the moral government of God, he may cherish his higher faculties and relations, where he may develope the attributes of a man, and render himself worthy of the dignity of that nature with which, in common with his fellows, his Creator has endowed him. To this has he come, and to this

3

is he entitled by Him who "Made him a little lower than the angels, and crowned him with glory and honor; and made him to have dominion over the work of his hands, and put all *things* under his feet. All sheep and oxen, yea, and the beasts of the field, the fowls of the air and the fish of the sea, and whatsoever passeth through the paths of the sea."

Now from this position, so befitting his nature and to which his title is not written upon parchment, but in every thought that burns within him, in every word he utters, and in every lineament of a man with which his Maker has impressed him,—from this position and these prerogatives, who will dare to tear him away? Who will dare to be his spoiler? Who will dare to thrust him down to chattelship and bruteism, slavery's doom? Who will dare to thrust him into that condition where an usurper upon the ownership of God may pollute his body and his soul with impunity,—may sunder every social tie of life, rob him of his Bible, seal up every source of knowledge, and interdict every command of his God; may, with the legally defined powers of his ownership, subject his quivering flesh to the lash and his spirit to despair. This, *this* is man-stealing! Hear it heaven and earth, THIS *is man-stealing!*

If done without law, it is man-stealing; if done under color of law, still it is man-stealing. In the sight of God the crime is the same, with the addition of conspiracy. Before heaven and earth the authors of that Bill are indictable for a conspiracy to commit one of the highest crimes for the punishment of which the law was made. 1. Tim. 1:9, 10. To those conspirators against God and against his helpless poor, shall be charged the mercenary crimes which will be committed under this terrible enactment, in that day when the scorners of God, the contemners of his law, and the crushed victims of their power shall be weighed together in an even scale. "Truly I am full of power by the spirit of the Lord, and of judgment and of might, to declare unto Jacob his transgressions and to Israel his sin. Hear this, I pray you, ye heads of the house of Jacob, and ye princes of the house of Israel that abhor judgment and pervert all equity. They build up Zion with blood, and Jerusalem with iniquity. The heads thereof judge for reward and the priests thereof teach for hire and the prophets thereof divine for money; yet will they lean upon the Lord and say, is not the Lord among us? No evil can come upon us." O, it is lamentable, when rulers are "a terror" to good works, and a praise to them that "do evil." In the enactment of this Bill, they have "framed mischief by a law." Well, the inflictions of their penalties may be borne; but surely no man who loves justice, fears God and believes in the retributions of eternity, will involve himself in this crime. Let them pour upon us, if they will, the vials of their wrath, but by the solemnities of the last day, let them not make us man-stealers. No, no; as we fear God this Bill must be disobeyed. Its inherent atrocity, its manifest hostility to the law of God makes disobedience to it an imperative duty.

REMARKS.

We have urged disobedience to this law for the recapture of fugitive slaves; and we have urged such disobedience, not as a capricious resistance of some heavy burden imposed upon us, but as a moral duty,—a duty solemnly required of God, because this law requires us to violate his law, and to stain ourselves with no ordinary guilt. And we urge it still. But let no one suppose for a moment that we urge rebellion. I know, indeed, that there are some who seem blind to the distinction between rebellion and disobedience to a law requiring us to do a wicked act. But that difference exists, nevertheless, and the distinction is clear. Daniel would not obey the law of Darius, but he would say, O king, live forever! And so we will not obey this wicked law, but to our Republican Government we will say, O king, live forever! Every law of the land gives to all the privilege, the right, not to disobey it and be tried for treason, but to disobey it and receive its prescribed penalty. If any one studiously refuse the former, but patiently submit to the latter, he is no rebel.

The authors of this Bill, traitors as they were to the high

trust to which they were elevated, were, nevertheless, clothed with official power. By disobedience to their unrighteous mandate, as far as in us lies, we will arrest the fearful results of their madness. From respect to the government, which they for the time represent, we will patiently submit to such penalties as they may inflict, trusting that God will support us under it, until, in his good providence, more worthy occupants of so high a trust shall undo the mischiefs which they have done. As to the extent and manner of disobedience to this law, I feel myself quite incompetent to advise. Indeed, no definite rule can be prescribed. The different circumstances under which individuals are placed in relation to it, must dictate the path of duty. And yet some general suggestions may be proper. As to the extent of disobedience I may say, in safety, that whenever and wherever and in just so far as it requires a violation of the gospel of Christ or the moral precepts of God, it should be disobeyed, and disobeyed with a firmness that knows no hesitation or change. As to the manner of disobeying it, some things are clear and obvious, others can only be suggested by the exigency of the case as it may arise.

Are you a magistrate, and should a kidnapper pursue, arrest and bring a fugitive from slavery before you, dare to lift yourself above the suborned truckling of a slavery-smitten judiciary, and be governed by your oath of office and by the Constitution, that great palladium of human rights, the provisions of which you are the especial and sworn protectors and guardians.

Are you an officer and commanded to execute it, refuse. Resign if you will; but if not, refuse, and say to the higher authorities, it was not in the contract of your office to turn a man-stealer, or to commit any other known and infamous crime.

If any officer, forgetting his higher allegiance to God, should undertake its execution and command your assistance, refuse. Perseveringly refuse to assist. In the simple majesty of righteousness and humanity, remonstrate and seek to dissuade such officer from thus aiding the guilty oppressor in his cruel work. Do all in your power without violence to protect the fugitive from seizure, or to hide him from pursuit. Hide him, feed him, comfort him in his peril and distress with all the fidelity, self-sacrifice and sympathy that you would if that poor, trembling fugitive from oppression were your Saviour, Jesus Christ; for it is for his *chosen* representative you do it.

But to all this it may be objected that the dangers of disobedience are such as not to be trifled with;—and so they are. They may not be trifled with, but they may, nevertheless, be looked soberly in the face, and be overcome. The authors of this law no doubt anticipated that its execution would be obstructed by all the humanity, all the conscience, all the religion of the country, and they have armed it accordingly. They have armed the executioners of this law with extraordinary powers to do an extraordinary work. The ordinary safeguards of the law are denied to the victim, for their especial accommodation. He may command what assistance he may need, under disproportionate and enormous penalties.

With those who take counsel of their fears, this objection will have weight. There is no want of liability or terror for him who dares to disobey its provisions. Cowards and traitors will find no want of apology; but with him who fears God, and whose integrity is not in the market, these considerations will weigh nothing. Such as are governed by sinister motives, will, of course, obey the law. Disobedience will be quite too costly to suit the standard of their ethics. But, let the warning of the Son of God be remembered,—"Fear not them that kill the body, and after that have no more that they can do. But I will forewarn you whom ye shall fear; fear Him, who, after He hath killed, hath power to cast both soul and body into hell. Yea, I say unto you, fear Him." With the wise, such a warning will be more than sufficient to counterbalance this objection. It shall console us to know that we are not the first who have found themselves hedged in between duty and danger;_ a position into which, first or last, God usually brings his children, that he may test their fidelity to himself and bring them forth as gold purified in the furnace.

But I submit whether there is not a relation which we sustain to this Bill, which, whether we obey it or not, involves us in its guilt. In this country the people are the government. Legislators are but the agents of the people. It is considered a sound maxim, that the principal is responsible for the agent. The immediate authors of this Bill are the legislators who passed it; the mediate authors are the people, whose agents they were.

"No Cæsar bears this sin alone,
A nation fills the guilty throne."

Nor let the fault be all laid upon the citizens of the South. If the free citizens of the North had hitherto done their duty on the subject of American Slavery, those unprincipled politicians from the North, who aided in passing this Bill, would never have done it. But they have been so long accustomed to sacrificing the rights of freedom at the shrine of the slave power, with your acquiescence, that they were emboldened to this last, rather startling, experiment upon your credulity and forbearance.

At the bidding of the slave power they have added State after State to the black stripes of our Union,—and you have acquiesced. At the bidding of the slave power, and in violation of solemn treaty, they have rent Texas from a sister republic, that they might give that vast area of freedom to its dark dominion,—and you have acquiesced. At the bidding of the slave power, they have waged a murderous and successful war of conquest upon Mexico,—and you have acquiesced.

At the perpetration of each of these successive acts of outrage and wrong, you have been startled and roused for a moment to a sense of their atrociety, but dazzled by the splendors of success, or bound by the trammels of party, you have offered no manly or persevering resistance. The fires of party strife have consumed every sober inquiry after righteousness and duty,—and you have acquiesced. From these successful experiments upon the easy virtue of the people, is it surprising that they should have ventured upon this last act? In view of all the past, why should they not now expect you to hold up your perhaps reluctant, but consenting hands, to be manacled, that you may be the conscienceless slaves of political *owners*, to catch and bind their human victims, and lay them upon the altar of the Southern Moloch where they worship?

But if, after all, I am mistaken—if for past delinquences you are not responspible for the existence of this Bill—yet I beg to assure you that you will be responsible for its long continuance. The mischief has been done by our permission, now let it be undone by our exertion. Repeal is a duty,—unconditional repeal. A duty pressing upon every free citizen of the North. We owe it to ourselves; its exactions are intolerable. We owe it to the suffering fugitives on whom this commission of "living death" has fallen. We owe it to our country, whose name this enactment has covered with reproach in the eyes of the civilized world. But above all, we owe it to God, against whose government and laws this Bill has arrayed us. Let other questions, which involve only pecuniary or mercenary considerations, be lost sight of in view of this great question of justice. Religiously are you bound to give your vote for no man, of whatever party or politics he may be, unless he is pledged to undo this great wrong which has been perpetrated in your name. Let repeal be our watchword. Let freemen rally as with one heart, and let this foul blot be wiped from the statute book of our nation.

CONCLUSION.

We have been long slumbering over the cruelties of slavery upon the millions of God's helpless poor. Perhaps God in his wisdom is now permitting us to feel its aggressions upon ourselves, that thereby we may be roused to duty. This overt and frenzied act of the slave power, may yet, through the overruling of Divine Providence, recoil with resistless power upon slavery itself. Let not those who fear God be dismayed. Let them buckle on the armor of God, and "stand in God's great might." He will "cause the wrath of man to praise him, and the remainder of wrath he will restrain." In all that afflicts us to-day, God will be glorified. The moral elements around us are in commotion; the horizon is lowering and dark. But let no man's faith falter. "God rides upon the storm," and "he stretcheth out his bow upon the cloud." "Why do the heathen rage, and the people imagine a vain thing? The kings of the earth set themselves, and the rulers take counsel together against the Lord, and against his anointed, saying, let us break their bands asunder, and cast away their cords from us. He that sitteth in the heavens shall laugh; the Lord shall have them in derision. Then shall he speak unto them in his wrath, and vex them in his sore displeasure. Yet have I set my King upon my holy hill of Zion." Upon that throne he will sit, and from that throne he will extend his sceptre, until the last fetter shall be broken, the last sigh shall be heaved, the last tear shall fall, and this aceldama of earth shall be changed into the paradise of God, and be filled with the glory of his reign.

I cannot better close this discourse than in the language of this beautiful Psalm.

Be wise, now, therefore, O ye kings;
Be instructed, ye judges of the earth.
Serve the Lord with fear,
And rejoice with trembling.
Kiss the Son, lest he be angry,
And ye perish from the way
When his wrath is kindled but a little.
———Blessed are all they
That put their trust in him.

www.ingramcontent.com/pod-product-compliance
Lightning Source LLC
LaVergne TN
LVHW011145110826
845150LV00008B/2516
9781418192068